# A GUST of WIND

# A GUST of WIND

Dr. Linda N. Cameron

Ordering Information:

For orders and inquiries, please contact:
1-888-404-1388
www.goldtouchpress.com
book.orders@goldtouchpress.com

Printed in the United States of America

A gust of wind is free, you see.

It has no roots like the grass or a tree.

But the grass of the land will dance and the leaves of trees will wave when the wind blows slowly by.

A gust of wind can't bloom like a
field of flowers, but it can cause
rain showers to loom across the sky

and spread seeds to create
new flowers nearby.

A gust of wind is not wet like
the sea or a lake,

yet it can make their waves
roll from dust to daybreak.

A gust of wind is not solid like stones or rocks,

but with many gusty knocks, the wind
can carve them out and make them
round all about.

Are you like a gust of wind, and free? You have no roots like the grass or a tree.

But you can dance like the
grass of the land and wave like
the leaves of the trees with
your hand.

You can't bloom like a field of flowers.
But you can scatter flower seeds and

pour enough water to meet their needs.

You're not wet like the sea or a lake but you can build a boat that will float over their waves from dust to daybreak.

You're not solid like stones or rocks but you can carve smiles across their tops.

So like a gust of wind,

you are free, you see!